THE UNADULTERATED CAT

THE UNADULTERATED CAT

A Campaign for Real Cats

TERRY PRATCHETT

cartoons by
GRAY JOLLIFFE

ORION

An Orion paperback
First published in Great Britain in 1989 as a paperback original
by Victor Gollancz Ltd
Revised Gollancz paperback edition 1992
This paperback edition published in 1999 by
Orion Books Ltd,
Orion House, 5 Upper St Martin's Lane, London WC2H 9EA

Text copyright © Terry and Lynn Pratchett 1989
Cartoons © Gray Jolliffe 1989

A CIP catalogue record for this book is available
from the British Library.

ISBN: 0 75283 715 X

Printed and bound in Great Britain by
Cox & Wyman Ltd, Reading, Berks

DEDICATION

All right, all right.
Time to come clean.
Despite the fact that
this book clearly states
that cats should have short names
you don't mind yelling
to the neighbourhood at midnight,
The Unadulterated Cat
is dedicated to:
Oedipuss.
They don't come much realer.

Contents

The Campaign for Real Cats

Far too many people these days have grown used to boring, mass-produced cats, which may bounce with health and nourishing vitamins but aren't a patch on the good old cats you used to get. The Campaign for Real Cats wants to change all that by helping people recognise Real Cats when they see them. Hence this book.

The Campaign for Real Cats is against fizzy keg cats.

All right. How can I recognise a Real cat?

Simple. Nature has done a lot of the work for you. Many Real cats are instantly recognisable. For example, all cats with faces that look as though they had been put in a vice and hit repeatedly by a hammer with a sock round it are Real cats. Cats with ears that look as though they have been trimmed with pinking shears are Real cats. Almost every non-pedigree unneutered tom is not only Real, but as it hangs around

11

the house it gets Realer and Realer until one of you is left in absolutely no doubt as to its Realness.

Fluffy cats are not *necessarily* unReal, but if they persist in putting on expressions of affronted dignity for the camera while advertising *anything* with the word 'purr-fect' in the associated copy they are definitely bringing their Realness into question.

Ah. So cats in adverts aren't Real?

Actually being in adverts doesn't make a cat unReal – it can't help it if someone plonks it down in some weird pyramid made of carpet and takes pictures of it peeping anxiously out of the hole – but its demeanour once there counts for a lot.

For example, if you put an unReal cat down in front

of a row of bowls of catfood it will obediently choose the one made by the sponsors of the ad even if all the others *haven't* got sump oil on them. A Real cat, on the other hand, will head for the most expensive regardless, pull it out onto the studio floor, eat it with guilty pleasure, try some of the others, trip up the cameraman and then get stuck behind the newsreaders' podium. Where it will be sick. And then, when its owners buy several large tins of the wretched stuff, it'll refuse to touch it ever again.

Real cats never wear bows (but sometimes they do wear bow-ties; see 'Cartoon Cats').

Or appear on Christmas cards.

Or chase anything with a bell on it.

Real cats don't wear collars. But Real cats often do wear dolls' clothes, and sit there also wearing an expression of furry imbecility while their brains do a complex radar scan of their surroundings and then they take a special kind of leap that gets them out of the mob cap, dress, apron and doll's pram all in one move.

Real cats are not simply self-possessed. Nor are they simply neurotic. They are both, at the same time, just like real people.

Real cats do eat quiche. And giblets. And butter. And

anything else left on the table, if they think they can get away with it. Real cats can hear a fridge door opening two rooms away.

There is some dispute about this, but some of the hardliners in the CRC say that Real cats don't go to catteries when their owners go on holiday, but are fed by a simple arrangement of bowls and neighbours. It is also held that Real cats don't go anywhere in neat wicker Nissen huts with dinky little bars on the front. Now, look. Schism and debate are of course the lifeblood of democracy, but I would *just* like to remind *some* of our more *enthusiastic* members of the great damage to the Campaign caused by the Flea Collar Discussion (1985), the Proprietary Cat Litter Row (1986) and what became rather disgracefully reported as the Great Bowl With Your Name On It Fracas (1987). As I said at the time, while of course the *ideal* Real cat eats its meals off an elderly saucer with remnants of the last meal still crusting the edge or, more typically, eats it off the floor just beside it, **a Real cat is what you are, not what is done to you**. Some of us may very well feel happier carting our cats around in a cardboard box with the name of a breakfast food on the side, but Real cats have an inbuilt distrust of white coats, can tell instantly when the vet is in prospect, and can erupt from even the stoutest cardboard box like a ICBM. This generally happens in dense traffic or crowded waiting rooms.

Despite the bad feeling caused by the Great Bowl With Your Name On It Fracas mentioned above, we should make it clear that Real cats *do* eat out of bowls with *PUSSY* written on the side. They'd eat out of them if they had the word **ARSENIC** written on the side. They eat out of *anything*.

Real cats catch things.

Real cats eat *nearly* all of everything they catch.

A Real cat's aim is to get through life peacefully, with as little interference from human beings as possible. Very much like real humans, in fact.

Can I be pedigree and a Real cat too?

Of course you can't. You're a human.

My cat, I mean.

Ah. A thorny one, this. Logically, simply knowing your great-granddad's name should not be a bar to enjoying the full rich life, but some of the Campaign's more *committed* members believe that a true Real cat should be in some doubt as to its own existence, let alone that of its parents.

We feel that this is an extreme view. It is true that many of us feel the quintessential Real cat looks like the survivor of a bad mincer accident, but if people are really going to go around judging a cat's Realness by looks and fur colour *alone*, then they must see that what they are working towards is a Breed in its own right ('And this Year's Supreme Champion is Sooty, by "Thatdamngreythingfromnextdoorsonthebirdtable*again*" out of "We Just Call Her Puss" of Bedwellty').

The point is that cats are different from dogs. A certain amount of breeding was necessary to refine dogs from the rough, tough, original stock to the smelly, fawning, dribbling morons* of uncertain temper that we see today. As they were turned into

---

*After considerable heated debate, the Committee wishes it to be made clear that this statement should *not* be taken to include, in order, small white terriers with an IQ of 150, faithful old mongrels who may be smelly but apparently we love him, and huge shaggy wheezing St Bernards who consume more protein in a day than some humans see in a year† but understand every word we say, no, really, and are like one of the family.

†The committee, failing despite tremendous pressure to have this phrase removed, haha, have asked it to be amended to 'has a healthy appetite for a dog of his age'. This refers to the way the huge snout drops like a bulldozer‡ and pushes a bowl the size of a washbasin clean across the kitchen, I suppose.

‡The committee can say what they like, but the Chairman, who indeed fully admits never to have experienced the joys and pleasures of dog ownership, intends never to do so, and fully accepts that there are houses where dogs and cats live in domestic harmony, has seen him eat.

anything that society felt at the time that it really wanted – self-powered earth-moving machines, for example, or sleeve ornaments – so the basic dogness was gradually diluted.

Yeah – he's real alright

Thus, your Real dog is far more likely to be a mongrel, except that the word is probably illegal these days, whereas all cats are, well, cats. More or less the same size, various colours, some fat, some thin, but still recognisably cats. Since the only thing they showed any inclination to do was catch things and sleep, no one ever bothered to tinker with them to make them do anything else. It's interesting to speculate on what they might have become had history worked out differently, though (see 'The Cats We Missed'). All that cats were bred for, in fact, was general catness. All cats are potentially Real. It's a way of life . . .

What has the Campaign for Real Cats got against dogs, then?

Nothing.

Oh, come on.

No, there are perfectly good, well-trained, well-behaved dogs who do not bark like a stuck record, or crap in the middle of footpaths, sniff groins, act like everyone's favourite on mere assumption, and generally whine, steal and grovel in a way that would put a 14th-century professional mendicant to shame. We recognise this.

Good.

There are also forgiving traffic wardens, tarts with hearts of gold, and solicitors that do not go on holiday in the middle of your complicated house purchase. You just don't meet them every day.

Getting started

We got a cat because we didn't like them much.

Our garden was debated territory between five local cats, and we'd heard that the best way to keep other cats out of the garden was to have one yourself.

A moment's rational thought here will spot the slight flaw in this reasoning. However, if you're predisposed to keep cats, rational thought has nothing to do with it. We've never met anyone who recalls waking up one day and thinking: 'This morning I will go shopping and buy some sprouts, one of those blue things for the lavatory, some baking foil – and, oh yes, a cat would be nice.'

Cats have a way of always having been there even if they've only just arrived. They move in their own personal time. They act as if the human world is one they just happened to have stopped off in, on their way to somewhere that is possibly a whole lot more interesting.

And what, when you come right down to it, do we know about them? Where did they come from? People say, well, evolution, it stands to reason. Why? Look at dogs. Dogs descended from wolves. You can tell.

Some dogs are alsatians, which is just a wolf in a collar, biding its time. And then there's all these smaller dogs, going down in size until you get the weird little ones with lots of Zs in their name which squeak and can get into pint mugs. The point is, you can *see* the evolution happening, all the way from hairy semi-wolves to bald yappy things bred to go up Emperors' sleeves or whatever.

You know that if civilisation suddenly stopped, if great clanking things from Alpha Centauri suddenly lurched out of the sky and spirited mankind away, the dogs would be about two meals away from becoming wolves again.

Or look at us. Some of the details might be a bit fiddly, but we – bright, civilised *us*, who know all about mortgages and non-stick saucepans and Verdi – can look back over our genetic shoulders and see a queue of stumbling figures going all the way back to little crouching shapes with hairy chests, no forehead and the intelligence of a gameshow audience.

Cats are different. On the one hand we have these great tawny brutes that sit yawning under the hot veldt sun or burning bright in jungles, and on the other there's these little things that know how to sleep on top of off-peak heaters and use cat doors. Not much in between, is there? A whole species divided, basically, between 500lbs of striped muscle that can bring down a gnu, and ten pounds of purr. Nowhere do we find the Piltdown Cat, the missing lynx. All right, there's the wild cat, but that just looks like your average domestic tabby who's been hit on the head with a brick and got angry about it. No, we must face it. Cats just turned up. One minute nothing, next minute Egyptians worshipping them, mummifying them, building tombs for them. No messing around with a spade in the sad bit of the garden behind the toolshed for your Pharaohs, not when 20,000 men and a load of log rollers were standing around idle.

Scientists working for the Campaign for Real Cats believe that, because of the Schrodinger experiments (*qv*), the whole question of where cats come from, and

We used to be as big as tigers but we had to shrink to fit through a cat-flap

how, is now totally meaningless, since there appear to be some cats that can travel quite painlessly across time and space, and therefore this means that the only place time we can be sure cats come from is *now*.

How to get a cat

1. Adverts in the Post Office

```
Five adorable tabby kittens
   Just ready to leave Mum
      Free to Good Home
      Please Phone .....
```

Yes. Please, *Please* Phone, because they're all big and fighting with one another and some of the males are beginning to take a sophisticated interest in Mum. Do not be fooled into believing that you will need to turn up bearing evidence of regular church-going and sober habits; good home in this case means anyone who doesn't actually arrive in a van marked

J Torquemada and Sons, Furriers.

If you answer the ad you'll find there's one kitten left.

There's always one kitten left. You spend ages trying to figure out what it was that made the previous four purchasers leave it behind. Eventually you will find out.

Nevertheless, Adverts in the Post Office are a good way of acquiring your basic cat.

2. Adverts in posh cat magazines

Pretty much like (**1**.) except that the word 'adorable' probably won't be used and the word 'free' *certainly* won't be used. Not to be contemplated by anyone on a normal income.

The cats acquired in this way are often very decorative, but if that's all you want a cat for then a trip to the nearest urban motorway with a paint scraper will do the business.

Pedigree cats talk a lot – catownerspeak for yowling softly – and tend to rip curtains. Being so highly bred, some of them are mentally unstable. A friend had an Arch-villains' cat (*qv*) which thought it was a saucepan. But, because it was very expensive and more highly bred than Queen Victoria, it thought it was a saucepan with *style*.

3. Buying a house in the Country

A very reliable way of acquiring a cat. It'll normally turn up within the first year, with a smug expression that suggests it is a little surprised to see you here. It doesn't belong to the previous occupants, none of the neighbours recognise it, but it seems perfectly at home. Why? It is very probably a *Schrodinger cat* (*qv*).

4. The Cats' Home

Another very popular source, especially just after Christmas and the summer holiday period, when their sales are on. Despite the fact that you can barely hear her on the phone for the background of yowling, the harassed young lady will probably take rather more pains than the average Post Office Advert cat seller to ensure you haven't actually got skinning knives in your pocket. Often no payment, just a voluntary donation – made at pistol point. You will be offered a variety of furry kittens, but the cat for you is the

one-year-old spayed female lurking at the back of the cage with a worried expression who will show her appreciation by piddling in the car all the way home.

5. Inheritance

These cats come with a selection of bowls, half a tin of the most expensive cat food on the market, a basket and a small woolly thing with a bell in it. They will then spend two weeks under the bed in the spare room. Try to get it out and it could be *you* in the hospital having skin from your buttocks grafted onto your arm.

Cats are not always inherited from dead people. If the previous owner is still alive, the Real cat will probably be accompanied by a list of its likes and dislikes. Throw it away. They're just fads anyway.

Try to avoid inheriting cats unless they come with a five-figure legacy, or at least the expectation of one.

6. Joint ownership

Do you know where your cat spends its time when it's not at home? It's worth checking with more distant neighbours that they don't have a cat with the same size and colouring. It can happen. We once knew two households who for years both thought they owned the same cat, which spent its time commuting between food bowls. A sort of *menagerie à trois*.

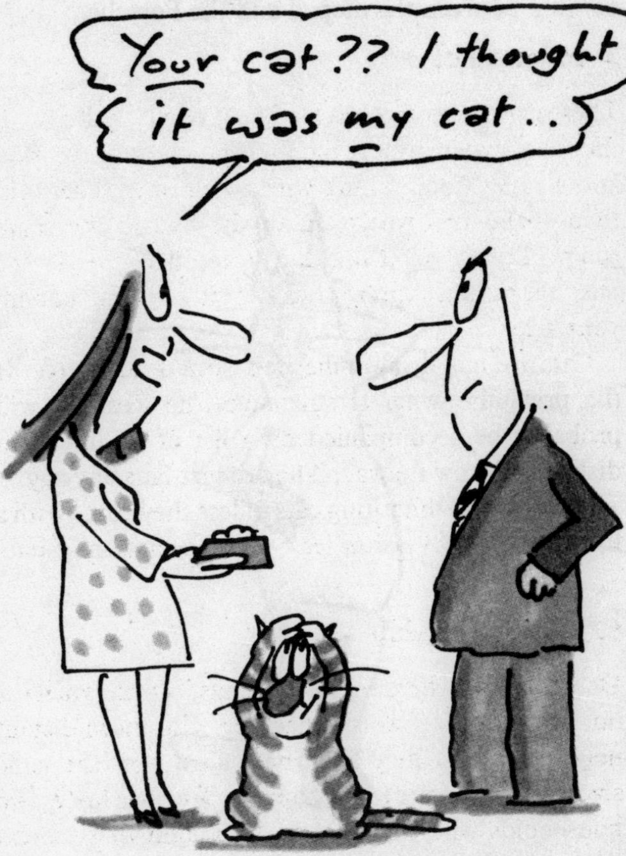
Your cat?? I thought it was my cat..

An interesting fact about acquiring cats is that the things are, by and large, either virtually free or very expensive. It's as if the motor industry had nothing between the moped and the Porsche.

Types of cat

Forget all the business about Blue Points and Persians. Real cats are likely to be:

1. Farm Cats

A dying breed. Once upon a time every decent barn supported a thriving, incestuous colony of them, depositing small nests of mewling kittens amongst the hay-bales, and there's still a few around. Worth getting if you can. They often look like flat-headed maniacs, but they've generally got a bit of sense. Not usually found on the kind of farms that are apparently made of extruded aluminium, but still scratching a living here and there.

2. Black Cats with White Paws

There *must* be a breed of these. Most Sub-Post Office cats (*qv*) are black cats with white paws. They are always called Sooty.

3. Neighbours' Cats

Usually grey, and often seen in the newly-seeded bit of the garden with a strained expression on their faces. Normally called Yaargeroffoutofityarbarstard (see 'Naming Cats').

4. Boot-faced Cats

They have fangs, crossed eyes, enough scars to play a noughts and crosses championship on, and ears like old bus tickets. They're invariably male. Boot-faced cats aren't born but made, often because they've tried to outstare or occasionally rape a speeding car and have been repaired by a vet who just pulled all the bits together and stuck the stitches in where there was room. Most Boot-faced cats are black. Strange but true.

5. Sort of Tabby Cats with a Bit of Ginger, But Sometimes In the Right Light You Could Swear There's a Hint of Siamese There

Your basic Real cat. Backbone of the country's cat population.

6. Factory Cats

Like farm cats, now ambling their way into history.

They were once kept because they did a useful job of work, but now they're often the subject of friction between management, who want them out because they don't fit in with the new streamlined image of United Holdings (Holdings) plc, and staff, who don't. Usually someone called Nobby or Dotinthecanteen smuggles in food for them. Some factory cats get to be quite famous and have their pictures in the staff newspaper when they retire. The picture always shows Nobby or Dotinthecanteen holding a saggy black-and-white cat which is staring at the camera with quiet, self-satisfied malevolence.

On retirement, they set up home with Dotinthecanteen but saunter down to the old firm occasionally and hang around while the working cats are going through a busy patch, telling them how much better they feel these days, wish they'd done it years ago, of course you lads don't know what it was like when Mr Morgan was manager, what a tartar he was, if he saw so much as a mouse doodah he went spare, you were kept at it in those days . . .

. . . and then they saunter back home, and have a nap.

7. Arch-villains' Cats

Always fluffy and white, with a diamond-encrusted collar. Other qualifications include the ability to yawn photogenically when the camera is on them and complete unflappability in the presence of people dropping through the floor into the piranha tank. We've all seen Arch-villains' cats.

However, it's not the easy life that it appears to be. For one thing, the people who design the megamillion underground yacht bunkers and missile bases in which the arch-criminals live never think to include a dirt box. If they did, it would be surrounded by landmines and have ingenious and unpleasant traps buried in it.

And Arch-villains' cats never use a cat door. This is because they know what happens to people who go through doors.

Arch-villains' cats are not Real. This is obvious to anyone who cares to examine the facts. Next Christmas, when once again the TV reminds you that a saviour was born on Earth and his name is James Bond, look closely at the sets. You will find there are no:

a) dead birds under the laser-driven spy splitting table

b) scratch marks on the megamissile control panel

c) forlorn squeaky toys lying around where people can trip over them

d) half-empty tins of suppurating cat food in the cryogenic unit.

Somehow, it's hard to imagine your average Arch-villain owning a Real cat (although some members have pointed out that many Arch-villains have leather gloves on their hands, and/or only one eye, so maybe they have Real cats at home they try to fondle after another hard day of holding the world to ransom.)

ARCH-VILLAIN'S CAT

Heh! heh!...

Ok hand it over - real cats don't use dynamite

8. Cartoon Cats

Usually black and white. And they often have an amusing speech impediment. If your cat can read newspapers, it is a Cartoon cat. If it can get hold of a stick of dynamite by simply reaching off screen, it is a Cartoon cat. If it wears a bow-tie, it's a Cartoon cat. If, when it starts to run, its legs pinwheel in the air for a humorous few seconds making *binka-binka-binka* noises, it is a Cartoon cat. If you are still uncertain, check to see whether the people next door have a bulldog called Butch who has spikes on his collar and is usually to be found dozing outside his kennel. If they have, you'll know what kind of cat you've got.

36

9. The Sub-Post Office Cat

A sub-species of Factory cat. Can be any colour in theory, are almost always black and white in fact. The significant characteristic of this breed is an ability to spread out when asleep, like a rubber bag full of mercury. They're gradually fading out, made redundant by the loss of the very shops they tended to inhabit and also by the Public Health laws, which are not drafted to accommodate the kind of animal that considers its natural role in life to go to sleep on a pile of sugar bags. I used to be taken into a shop where a Sub-Post Office cat used to sleep *in* the dog biscuit sack. You'd reach in to pinch a bikkie and there'd be all this fur. No one seemed to mind. (Whatever happened to those dog biscuits? They were *real* dog biscuits, not the anaemic things you get in boxes today; they were red and green and black and came in various interesting shapes. The black ones tasted of charcoal. That's modern times for you. Our grandparents had oil lamps and gas lights to look back to, we've got dog biscuits. Even the nostalgia isn't what it was.)

10. Travelling Cats

Oscar's 2,000 Mile Purr-fect Trip

says the heading in the local paper. Or something like that. At least once every year. *In every local paper*. It's a regular, like 'Row Over Civic Site' or 'Storm As Schools Probe Looms'.

So many stories like this have turned up that researchers from the Campaign for Real Cats have been, well, researching. The initial suspicion was that here was a hitherto unknown breed of Real cat, possibly a sideshoot of the now almost extinct Railway cat. It'd be nice to think that there was today an Airline cat, although perhaps not, because warming though the idea is, the thought is bound to occur to you at 30,000 feet that it's probably got a favourite sleeping area somewhere on the plane and it is possibly somewhere in the wiring. Or perhaps there is now a Lorry cat undreamed of by T. S. Eliot. *Felis Freuhaf*, an international creature, loitering in the cabs of the world and growing fat on Yorkie Bars. Or it could be further proof of the Schrodinger theory, since from a quantum point of view distance cannot be said to exist and all this apparent space between things is just the result of random fluctuations in the matter matrix and shouldn't be taken seriously.

The astonishing truth has not been suspected, possibly because not many people in this country have more than one local paper. But, from hundreds of cuttings sent in by Campaign members, it finally emerged.

They're all the same cat. Not the same *type* of cat. The same *cat*.

It's a smallish black and white tom. Never mind

about the variety of names, which are only of significance to humans, although interestingly the name Oscar *does* seem to crop up rather a lot. Careful analysis of dozens of pictures of the Travelling cat blinking in the flashlight's glare has proved it.

It appeared to do a minimum of 15,000 miles last year, much of it in car engine compartments, where only its piteous mewling alerts the driver when he stops off for a coffee.

Confirmation will not be achieved until Oscar has been tracked down by researchers armed with a truck-load of painful equipment, but the current, rather interesting, theory is that what initially appears to be

OSCAR

ANYWHERE

this piteous mewling is in fact a stream of directions on the lines of 'left here, I said *left, left* you twerp, all right, keep going until we get to the trading estate and then you can pick up the A370 . . .'

Oscar is, in fact, trying to get somewhere. The process is a bit hit and miss, and possibly he has underestimated the size of the country and the number of vehicles in it, but he's keeping at it. Certainly, in the best tradition of Real cats everywhere, he's doing anything rather than get out and walk.

Incidentally, some recent press cuttings suggest that Oscar has given birth to kittens in a car engine compartment. This makes a tiny hole in part of the theory – nothing that a reasonable grant couldn't plug – but leads to the intriguing thought that perhaps there will be a new race of Travelling cats after all. And all growing up believing that home is something that you can only get to by climbing inside noisy tin things that move at 70 mph.

Perhaps lemmings started out like this.

In the course of this work one researcher did turn up a fascinating anecdote about St Eric, the 4th-century Bishop of Smyrna, believed by many to be the true patron saint of Real cats. While on his way to deliver an epistle he is said to have tripped over a cat and shouted, 'In faith, I wysh that Damned Mogge *wode* Goe Awae and Never Come Backe!'

It was a small black and white tom, according to contemporary accounts.

11. The Green, Bio-Organic, Whole Earthbox Cat

This type has been around since the Sixties at least. You may recall stories about cats fed on sweetcorn and avocados (no, really; a local pet shop sells vegetarian dog food). And, indeed, if the rest of the household is on the path of inner wholeness it rather lets the whole holistic business down to have tins of minced innards in the fridge.

We had vegan* friends who handled the cat food

This is Timmy—he's a vegetari....

*If you meet a vegan it's bad form to give them the famous four-fingered V sign and say 'Live long and prosper'. That's for vulcans. Vegans are the ones with the paler complexions who can't disable people by touching them gently on the neck.

tin in the same way that people at Sellafield handle something that's started to tick. In the end, they worked out a vegetarian diet with the occasional treat of fish. Their cat was a young Siamese. It thrived on the stuff. Of course it did. It used to go out and hang around the organic goat shed, and ate more rats and mice than its owners had hot dinners, which wasn't hard. But it was very understanding about it, and never let them know. We occasionally saw it trotting over the garden with something fluffy in its mouth, and it used to give us looks of conspiratorial embarrassment, like a Methodist minister caught enjoying a pint.

In fact cats are naturally Green animals. After all:

a) No cats have ever used aerosol sprays. Sprays, maybe, but not aerosol ones. The ozone layer is perfectly safe from cats.

b) Cats don't hunt seals. They would if they knew what they were and where to find them. But they don't, so that's all right.

c) The same with whales. People might have fed whales *to* cats, but the cats didn't know. They'd have been just as happy with minced harpooner.

d) Antarctica? Cats are quite happy to leave it alone.

Of course, they have their negative points:

a) All cats insist on wearing real fur coats. . . .

Naming cats

All cats, we know, have several names. T. S. Eliot came nowhere near to exhausting the list, though. A perfectly ordinary cat is likely to be given different names for when:

a) you tread on it

b) it's the only animal apparently able to help you in your enquiries as to the mysterious damp patch on the carpet and the distressing pungency around the place

c) your offspring is giving it a third-degree cuddle

d) it climbed up the loft ladder Because It Was There and then, for some reason, decided to skulk right at the back of all the old boxes, carpets, derelict Barbie houses, etc, and won't be coaxed out, and then when you finally drag it out by the scruff of its neck it scratches your arm in a friendly way and takes a beautiful leap which drops it through the open hatchway and onto the stepladder,

which then falls over, leaving you poised
above a deep stairwell on a winter's
afternoon while the rest of the family are
out.*

*All right, not perhaps a name you'd use *every* day, but best to
have one ready, just in case, because when you're leaning
against the freezing cold water tank trying to staunch the
blood with a priceless antique copy of *Bunty* you don't want to
have to tax the imagination as well.

It's an interesting fact that fewer than 17% of Real cats end their lives with the same name they started with. Much family effort goes into selecting one at the start ('She looks like a Winifred to *me*'), and then as the years roll by it suddenly finds itself being called Meepo or Ratbag.

Which brings us to the most important consideration in the naming of cats: never give a cat a name you would mind shouting out in a strained, worried voice around midnight while banging a tin bowl with a spoon. And stick to something short.

That being said, most common names for Real Cats are quite long and on the lines of **Yaargeroffout-ofityarbarstard**, **Mumthere'ssomethingORRIBLE-underthebed**, and **Wellyoushouldn'tofbinstanding-there**. Real Cats don't have names like Vincent Mountjoy Froufrou Poundstretcher IV, at least for long.

The chosen name should also be selected for maximum carrying power across a busy kitchen when, eg, a bag full of prime steak starts moving stealthily towards the edge of the table. You need a word with a cutting edge. **Zut!** is pretty good. The Egyptians had a cat-headed goddess called Bast. Now you know why.

Illnesses

Real cats are subject to the same illnesses that unReal cats get, although by and large Real cats tend towards rude health – not counting, of course, the occasional little intestinal problem which could happen to anyone.

However, there are several specifically Real cat ailments:

Impatient legs

Weird, this. We had a cat who suffered badly. The vet couldn't explain it. The cat could climb trees, ladders,

IMPATIENT LEGS

anything, it was as agile as you please, but when it tried to run fast it was all okay until *its back legs tried to pass*. Then it'd get so embarrassed at the sight of its own rear end coming past on the fast lane it would stop and wash its paws in shame. If it forgot itself and really made a dash for it, it was likely to end up facing the wrong way.

Flypaper

Well, okay. Not common. But one of the biggest cat ailments we've ever faced. Ho – we said – let's be ecological, remember the ozone layer, have no truck with flysprays, whatever happened to good old-fashioned flypaper. Finally found some, after shop-keepers made mad faces ('man here wants flypaper, keep smiling, desperately signal assistant to call police, will soon be asking for crinoline hoops and a pound of carbide crystals'). Got it home, hung it up in open window, bluebottles soon stuck fast like small angry currants, hooray, paper swayed in breeze, Real Cat *leapt* . . .

Real Cat becomes spinning furry propeller. Paper snaps, cat falls out of window, begins massive chase across gardens as it tries to escape from unwound paper trailing behind it, finally brought to earth in distant shrubbery because only one leg now capable of movement.

Panic, panic, where box flypaper came in? This is

1980s, paper bound to be covered with Polydibi-trychloroethylene-345, oh god, cat now immobile with terror inside kitchen towel. Fill huge bowl with warm water, drop cat in, swish it around, cat doesn't protest, oh god, perhaps Polydibitrychloro-ethylene-345 already coursing through tiny veins. Change water, rinse again, brisk towelling down, put cat on path in sun.

Cat looks up, gives mildly dirty look, turns and walks slowly up garden, lifting each paw one at a time and giving it a shake, like C. Chaplin.

After all that it was a bit of a let-down to find the flypaper box at the bottom of the waste bin and discover that, far from being the complex chemical trap we'd feared, it was just some jolly ecological plain sticky paper.

Sitting and hiccupping gently (with the occasional burp)

We've always put this down to voles.

Eating grass

Never been sure that this is a symptom of illness. It probably comes under the heading of Games: 'Hey, I'm being watched, let's eat some grass, that'll worry them, they'll spend half an hour turning the house upside down looking for the cat book, haha.'

Lorries

Can be fatal. But not always. We knew a cat who regarded motorised vehicles as sort of wheeled mice, and leapt out on them. It had so much scar tissue that its fur grew at all angles, like a gooseberry. Even its stitches had stitches. But it still lived to a ripe old age, terrorising other cats with its one good eye and forever jumping out at lorries in its sleep. It was probably looking for one that squeaked.

However healthy the cat, there will come a time when it needs a Pill. Oh, how we nod and look like respectable, concerned cat owners as the vet hands us the little packs (one grey one every five days and then a brown one after ten days, or was it the other way round?). And once we were all innocent and thought, the cat food smells like something off the bottom of a pond anyway. Real cat can't possibly notice if we crumble the damn things up a bit and mix them in . . .

As we get wiser, of course, we learn that the average Real cat has taste buds that make the most complex computer-driven sensory apparatus look like a man with a cold. It can spot an alien molecule a mile off (we tried halving the suspect food and adding more from the tin, and kept on doing it until it was like that famous French chemical experiment with the weird water and everything, there surely couldn't have been any pill *left*, but Real cat knew).

52

Next comes the realist phase ('after all, from a purely geometrical point of view a cat is only a tube with a door at the top').

You take the pill in one hand and the cat in the other . . .

Er . . .

You take the pill in one hand and in the other you take a large kitchen towel with one angry cat head poking out of the end. With your third hand you prise open the tiny jaws, insert the pill, clamp the jaws shut and, with your fourth hand, tickle the throat until a small gulping noise indicates that pill has gone down.

You wish.

It hasn't gone down. Because it's just gone sideways. Real cats have a secret pouch in their cheeks for this sort of thing. A Real cat can take a pill, eat a meal, and then spit out the slightly damp pill with a noise which, if this was a comic strip, would probably be represented as *ptooie*.

It is important to avoid the third stage, which basically consists of Man, Beast and Medicine locked in dynamic struggle and ought to be sculpted rather than described (as in Rodin's 'Man Giving Pill to Cat').

The fourth stage is up to you. Usually by now the cat is displaying such a new lease of life that the treatment might be said to have worked. Grinding the pill up with a bit of water and spooning it in sometimes does the trick. A fellow Real cat owner says powdering the wretched object – the pill, not the cat, although by stage four you'll entertain any idea – mixing it with a little butter and smearing it on a paw is a sure-fire method, because the cat's ancient instinct is to lick itself clean. Close questioning suggested that he hadn't actually *tried* this, just deduced it from theoretical studies (he's an engineer, so that explains it). Our view is that an animal that will starve and asphyxiate before taking its medicine won't have any trouble with a grubby paw.

Feeding cats

For centuries the idea of feeding cats was as unbelievable as squaring the circle. So was feeding chickens, for that matter. They just hung around, making their own arrangements; the whole point about having them was to keep down vermin and generally tidy up the place. Dogs got fed, cats got scraps. If they were lucky.

We all know what it's like now.

Feeding Real cats follows a pattern as changeless as the seasons.

1. Real cat turns up its nose at gold-plated tinned stuff recommended by woman on television.

2. Out of spite, you buy some down-market own-brand stuff whose contents you really wouldn't want to know about (after all, considering what can be put in beefburgers and sausages . . . no, you really wouldn't want to know about it . . .) Cat wolfs it down, licks empty plate across floor.

3. Out of relief, next shopping trip you buy a dozen tins of the humming stuff.

4. Cat turns up nose at it after one meal. This is a cat, you understand, that will eat dragonflies and frogs.

Having for some time watched what cats *will* eat, then I can safely say that any enterprising manufacturer who markets a cat food made of steak, half-thawed turkey, grass, flies, crumbs from under tables,

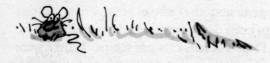

frogs and voles will be on to a winner. At least for one meal.

The alternative, of course, is hunting. The theory is that a well-fed cat is better at hunting than a hungry one. The reasoning is that a plump and full cat will be more content to lie in wait for the things that need guile and patience to catch – dragonflies, frogs, robins, that sort of thing – while a hungry one will merely dash about the place filling up on ordinary rats and mice. It's not certain who first advanced this view, but it's an evens bet that they probably had fur and whiskers.

Real cats don't hunt for food, but because they love you. And, because they love you, they realise that for some reason you have neglected to include in your house all those little personal touches that make it a home, and do their best to provide them. Headless shrews are always popular. For that extra splash of colour, you can't beat miniature sets of innards. For best effect such items should be left somewhere they won't be found for some days, and can have a chance to develop a personality of their own.

We had friends in an isolated cottage who had one cat, a big fat boot-faced thing, which'd never turn a paw to hunting despite the hordes of rats that besieged the property on every side. So they got another one, a sleek white young female who strode off into the long grass every day with a purposeful air. But, strangely, never came back with anything. Even odder, the resident huge cat began to hunt and turned up every day with something resembling a draught excluder in its mouth, or was found sitting proudly beside a miniature rodent Somme on the doorstep. Aha, they thought, spurred on by competition he's finally got cracking.

What they eventually found out, as any Real cat

owner would suspect, was that he was waylaying the female as she approached the house and glaring at her until she dropped the booty, then picking it up and carrying it the rest of the way. When it came to delegation, that was a cat who got someone else to write the book.

Training and disciplining the Real cat

Always a tricky one, this, for Real cat owners, who tend to be the types to whom parade-ground shouting and the legendary rolled-up newspaper does not come easily (if it did, they would then be one of those people with huge bounding dogs who do whatever they damn well please in a huge, jolly way to distant strains of 'Prince! NO! I said NO! **PUT IT DOWN! This minute! Prince! NO!**' etc).

What it really boils down to is the difference between Inside and Outside (cf. 'Hygiene'). Most Real cats cotton on to the idea fairly quickly. Most Real cats, after all, are bright enough to know that a dry box in a corner of the kitchen is a better bet than a flower bed when the wind is blowing straight from Siberia. Their mothers apparently educate them, though the considerable attention paid to this has been unable to fathom exactly how this is done, apart from persistently moving them around in a slightly neurotic game of kitten chess. Possibly the kittens are taken to some secret cat school where they are shown diagrams. (It's amazing how self-possessed and intelligent cats turn out to be when brought up by their mothers. We've been brought up by our mothers for millennia, and look at us. If Romulus and Remus had been reared by a cat instead of a wolf, Rome would be a different place today.)*

Beyond that, you can't teach cats to do anything. No, not a thing. You might think you can, but that is because you've misunderstood what's going on. *You* think it's the cat turning up obediently at the back door at ten o'clock on the dot for its dinner. From the cat's point, a blob on legs has been trained to take a tin out of the fridge every night.

*It'd have better lavatories, for a start.

Discipline – once you get beyond all the blanco and school traditions – means, If You Don't Do What I Want I'll Hit You. One problem here, of course, is that a cat is a hard animal to hit. A dog is always amenable to the famous rolled-up newspaper, whereupon it can go into the sorrowful grovelling, whining and sighing routine that would get a human actor booed off the stage. Hitting a cat is like walloping a furry glove full of pins, and doesn't make a blind bit of difference anyway. A relative who will remain unidentified until the RSPCA Statute of Limitations runs out always reckoned that a half-brick thrown the length of a garden* was necessary even to get a cat to pay attention. Distasteful though it may seem, however, there are times when even a Real cat owner feels it necessary to Take Action. Here are some options:

The Great Ballistic Clod of Earth

. . . which is the first thing to hand when you're digging† and you see, out of the corner of your eye, the guilty crouching shape as it sits among the

---

*If St Francis of Assisi had prided himself on his broccoli, and saw the last little seedling turning yellow because of the ministrations of Itsthatsoddingtomfromnextdoor, he would have done the same thing.

†Apart from the garden fork, and this isn't that type of book.

cabbages and peas.* The GBCoE is the rubber bullet of garden preservation, designed to chastise without actual death. The approved method is to hit ground zero about eighteen inches from the culprit, the resultant short sharp shower of shrapnel causing it to leap two feet vertically and suffer acute intestinal distress for the rest of the day.

The trouble is, though, that the cat soon works out that you are a typical Real cat owner, ie, a soft touch, and realises that if it calls your bluff, your ferocious stance will melt and you'll just run grumbling to the United Nations. The four cats that turn our garden into a vegetable Jonestown every Spring have realised this, and sit demurely among the whizzing clods visibly thinking 'Why is the funny man jumping up and down like that? And why is his aim so bad?'

*Or the cauliflowers and leeks, naturally.

Deep Pits with Spikes at the Bottom

Don't think this hasn't been discussed.

Pushing them into the Pond

Just occasionally Life gets It Right, like the time the sly alsatian from up the road decided to crap in the middle of Real cat owner's driveway just when Real cat owner was coming round the corner with a large onion in his hand.

Even better, though, was Real cat owner waking up from a doze on the lawn to find the current incumbent of the local Mad Feral Tom slot on the edge of the goldfish pond, staring intently at what remained of the inhabitants. Real cat owner quickly learns that it is, in fact, possible to go from a recumbent position into a full-length dive. But life's a strange thing. Cats can walk on water. I'll – that is, Real cat owner'll – swear MFT leapt *off the surface*.

Where was Real cat, obtained you will remember in order to keep other cats out of the garden, when this was going on? Asleep on chair in kitchen, as is always the case. Anyway, felt so bad about the way he wandered off, gave him free meal of sardines later.

Punishment has no effect on Real cats. This is because *Real cats don't associate the punishment with the crime*. As far as they're concerned, shouting, slippers on a low trajectory and being talked to in a loud, patient voice are all manifestations of the general weirdness of the blobs. All you have to do to survive it is cower a wee bit and look big-eyed, and then get on with your life.

Psychological Warfare

You might as well challenge a centipede to an arse-kicking contest. You always start off ignoring the animal, and end up treating it with added kindness because it appears to be suffering from something.

Calling in the Mafia

Only in the worst case. It's beset with difficulties anyway, because:

1. They're not in the phone book.

2. It's expensive. Four small concrete boots still cost twice as much as two large ones, it's a bit like children's shoes.

3. It is almost impossible to get a horse's head into a cat basket.

Games cats play

No, this isn't all that stuff with the bells and catnip-filled calico mice. Cats only play with special cat toys for about two minutes, when you're around, in order that you don't get depressed and stop buying them food.

The thing to remember here is that cats only *appear* to be solitary animals, forever mooching around the place by themselves. In fact all cats are plugged into this sort of huge feline consciousness which transcends time and space and, in its own mind, a cat is constantly competing and measuring itself against all cats who have ever existed anywhere. It's as if Steve Davis wasn't simply competing against another man in a dicky bow, but against every snooker player throughout history, right back to the first proto-hominid who needed a really mind-numbing way of spending his evenings.

Cats have subtle, intellectual games.

Cat chess

This needs, as the playing area, something the size of a small village. Up to a dozen cats can take part. Each cat selects a vantage point – a roof, the coal house wall, a strategic corner or, in quiet villages, the middle of the road – and sits there. You think it's just found a nice spot to sun itself until you realise that *each cat can see at least two other cats*. Moves are made in a sort of high-speed slink with the belly almost touching the ground. The actual rules are a little unclear to humans, but it would seem that the object of the game

Cat chess.

is to see every other cat while remaining unseen yourself. This is just speculation, however, and it may well be that the real game is going on at some mystically higher level unobtainable by normal human minds, as in cricket.

Wet cement

A popular and simple cat game which archaeologists have found is as old as, well, wet cement. It consists of finding some wet cement and then running through it. There are degrees of skill, of course. Most marks are scored by running through cement which, while still being wet enough to take a pretty pattern of paw marks, is too far set for the builder to smooth them out.

The Builder's Nice New Pile of Clean Sand

This is similar to Wet Cement, only, er, not quite.

Offside

Offside is a cat game similar to Zen archery, in that it is not what is actually done but the style in which it is achieved that really matters. It consists simply of persistently being on the wrong side of a door, and goes on for as long as human tolerance will stand and then a bit longer. A straightforward little game, only marginally more complex than the old favourite, **Staring at the fridge**.

However, there are degrees of complexity, and a skilled player of **Offside** will naturally choose locations which, while preternaturally difficult for humans to get to, will be soup and nuts for the cat to get away from.

𝕿𝖍𝖊 𝕷𝖔𝖈𝖐𝖊𝖉 𝕲𝖊𝖗𝖇𝖎𝖑 𝕸𝖞𝖘𝖙𝖊𝖗𝖞 is a case in point.

Neighbour went away for holiday, leaving complex instructions *re* watering of garden, etc, but not to worry about the pullulating colony of gerbils in the dining room because distant relative Mrs Thing would drop in every day or two to keep an eye on them.

Night comes, but not accompanied by Real cat. Familiar midnight performance, standing outside back door banging plate with spoon and calling out cat's name in squeaky voice, you know how you do, in tones that you hope will attract cat while not waking neighbours. Fancy takes hold, fears of lorries, foxes, traps float across mind.

Answer rises with dreadful inevitability, like boiling milk. Take torch, put on dressing gown, pad through dewy grass to picture-window of neighbour's house. Cat is sitting dribbling on dining table, watching vibrating gerbil colony, which is going mad. Treadmills are squeaking frantically in the night.

Mrs Thing must have been and Real cat, always on the look out for new experiences, must have wandered into the house while the door was open.

Do what any Real cat owner does in these circumstances, but cat takes no notice of shouts and threats. Run around house looking for open window, but all has been sealed tight against burglars, ie, self.

Run back home. Wasn't listening properly to instructions, can't remember who Mrs Thing really is or where she lives.

Also, how long is a day or two? Gerbils seem to live indefinitely in Spaceship Gerbil, with huge food hopper and nothing to do but make more gerbils. Whereas cat eats with knife, fork and rammer and has hair-trigger appetite. How long can it last? How long can it last on gerbil?

Run back again, try garage door, miraculously been left open, *bang clong thud* in the misty dawn, Neighbourhood Watchers probably already have digit poised to press the third 9, police will arrive *deedahdeedah*, pull the other one, chummy, it's got bells on, neighbours summoned from hotel bed in Majorca, may or may not corroborate story, will have crime record, family shunned in street, We Are All Guilty . . .

Still door from garage into house itself. Locked. Wonder if situation justifies breaking in *but* neighbours away for fortnight, can't leave house with broken door, will have to get carpenter, etc, in, and he won't be able to come along for probably three weeks.

Look under door. See cat paws. Cat has turned up to watch entertainment. Peer through keyhole, all dark, key still in there . . .

Sudden flashback. *Eagle* comic, c. 1958. Tips for Boys No. 5: Beating the Burglar. Apparently miscreants push newspaper under door, twiddle key in lock with special key twiddler, key drops down onto paper, paper pulled back under door.

Home again, grab paper, tweezers, three-in-one oil, run back, twiddle, twiddle, key drops down, pull paper, there is key. Unbelievable but true.

Unlock door. Cat no longer visible. Run from room to room. Thousands of frightened eyes stare from tower tenement block that is gerbil colony, even sex isn't so interesting as watching damp, crazed, dressing-gown wearer charging around room. Search under beds. Look out of window, see Real cat strolling down drive.

Neighbour had turned water off before going on holiday. This had meant lifting floorboard in washroom. This had left easy access to huge draughty space under bungalow, with dozens of entry holes for inquisitive cats. Slam board down, stamp heavily, break tap . . .

Another old favourite among cat games is:

Being Good

Doesn't sound much like a game, but the most important rule about Being Good is that the cat should *be good in such a way as to cause maximum trouble to its owner who can't however give it a thump because it is manifestly Being Good*. We had a cat who would, very occasionally, catch some small, inoffensive and squeaky creature and leave it on the scraper mat outside the door. You know – those flat scrapers that are rather like a chip slicer, with lots of little blades sticking up? And, of course, first thing in the morning you don't look down as you step out . . . This might, of course, be a Real cat's way of food preparation. But we knew, and it knew, that in reality it was Being Good.

Schrodinger [‘And *I* say you *must* have left a window open’]cats

All cats are now Schrodinger cats. Once you understand that, the whole cat business falls into place.

The original Schrodinger cats were the offspring of an infamous quantum mechanics experiment of the 1930s (or possibly they weren't the original ones. Possibly there were no *original* ones.)

Everyone's heard of Erwin Schrodinger's famous thought experiment. You put a cat in a box with a bottle of poison, which many people would suggest is about as far as you need go. Then you add a little bottle-smashing mechanism which may – or may *not* – smash the bottle; it all depends on random nuclear thingummies being given off by some radioactive material. This is also in the box. It is a large box. *Now*, according to quantum theory, the cat in the box is both a wave and a particle . . . hang on, no. What it *is*, because of all these quantums, is in a state of not actually being either alive or dead,* but both and neither at the same time, until the observer lifts the lid

*ie, uncertain. Because of Heisenberg's Uncertainty Principle.

and, by the act of observation, sort of *fixes* the cat in space/time etc. He's either looking at a candidate for the sad patch, or a spitting ball of mildly-radioactive hatred with bits of glass in it. The weird part about it is that, before the lid is lifted, not only the cat's future but also its immediate past are both undecided. It might *have had been* dead for five minutes, for example.

That's the story that got into the textbooks, anyway.* Less well known is the work by a group of scientists who failed to realise that Schrodinger was talking about a 'thought experiment'†, and did it. Box, radioactive source, bottle of poison, everything. And the cat, of course.

They left out one important consideration, though. While the observer might not know what was going on, the cat in the box damn well would. We can assume that if the prospect of hanging concentrates the mind, then the inkling that, any minute now, some guy in a white coat is going to lift the lid and there's a fifty-fifty chance that you are dead *already*,

---

*If you can believe it. It's like the one about one twin staying here and the other going off to Sirius at the speed of light and coming back and finding his brother is now a grandfather running a huge vegetable wholesale operation in Bradford. How does anyone *know*? Has anyone met them? What was it like on Sirius, anyway?

†One that you can't do, and which won't work.

80

If it weren't for the cat food factor I'd say you were only a figment of my imagination
101 THINGS to do with a dead cat

does wonders for the brain. Spurred by this knowledge, and perhaps by all the quantums floating around the laboratory, the cat nipped around a corner in space-time and was found, slightly bewildered, in the janitor's cupboard. Evolution is always quick to exploit a new idea, however, and this novel way of getting out of tricky situations was soon passed on to its offspring. It had a large number of offspring. Given its new-found talent, this is not surprising.

The important gene was so incredibly dominant that now many cats have a bit of Schrodinger in them. It is characterised by the ability *to get in and out of locked boxes*, such as rooms, houses, fridges, the thing you swore you put it in to take it to the vet, etc. If you threw the cat out last night, and this morning it's peacefully asleep under your bed, it's a Schrodinger cat.

There is a school of thought which says there is in fact a sort of negative Schrodinger gene. Whereas your full-blown Schrodinger can get in and out of the most unusual places there are cats, it has been pointed out, that would find it difficult to get out of a hoop with both ends open. These are the cats that you normally see, or rather, you normally *hear* behind fridges, in those dead little areas behind kitchen

storage units, in locked garages and, in one case known to us, inside the walls (dreadful Edgar Allan Poetic visions led to a hole being knocked into the cavity a little way from the noise, which of course caused the cat – definitely a Real cat – to retreat further from the noise; it came out 24 hours later, dragged by the scent of a plate of food). But we are inclined to believe that this is not so and that these are merely examples of *Offside* (see 'Cat Games').

However, this ability, which most Real cats' owners will have noticed (and what about when they're missing for a couple of days, eh, and come back well fed? Have they just been panhandling round the neighbours, or did they nip along to next Wednesday to enjoy the huge relieved 'welcome-back' meal you gave them?), leads on to interesting speculation about:

The cat in history

The books will tell you that cats evolved from civet ancestors about 45 million years ago, which was definitely a good start. Get as much distance between yourself and the civets as possible, that was the motto of the early cats. The civet cat has been a very nervous animal ever since it discovered that you can, er, derive civetone* from it and use it in scent. Exactly how this is done I don't know and do not wish to research. It's probably dreadful. Oh, all right, I'll have a look.

It is.†

So, the story goes, the cat family pushed on with the evolving as fast as possible, going in for size, speed and ferocity. There's nothing like the fear that you might be mistaken for a civet for giving jets to your

---

*A 17-member ring ketone, according to my dictionary, as opposed to the mere 15-membered muscone from the musk deer. Does the civet feel any better for knowing this? Probably not.

†Who invents these scents, anyway? There's a guy walking along the beach, hey, here's some whale vomit, I bet we can make scent out of this. Exactly how likely do you think this is?

genes, especially when you know it's only a matter of millennia before your actual proto-hominids start wandering around the Holocenic landscape with a bottle, a knife and a speculative look in their eyes.

They also spread out a bit but missed Australia, which had just gone past on the Continental Drift; this explains why the rats grew so big. Some got stripes, some tried spots. One well known early variety developed its very own do-it-yourself can opener a hundred thousand years before cat food came in tins, and died of being too early to take advantage of this.

And then, suddenly, small versions started to turn up and go mee-owp, mee-owp at people.

Consider the situation. There you are, forehead like a set of balconies, worrying about the long-term effects of all this new 'fire' stuff on the environment, you're being chased and eaten by most of the planet's large animals, and suddenly tiny versions of one of the worst of them wanders into the cave and starts to purr.

More amazing yet, it didn't get et.

Dogs you can understand. They're pack creatures, humans are just another, brighter, pack leader. Dogs are handy for helping you run down things that are faster than you are. But cats – well, from Early Man's point of view, cats are good for nothing.

The first cat to approach the cave survived, in fact, on sheer surprise value. It was the first animal the man had ever seen that wasn't either running away or bounding towards him and dribbling. It *liked* him.

And the reason it felt this way was that *the cat already knew that humans liked cats.*

Here was a household in the country. Households in the country attract cats. It's one of the fundamental wossnames of Nature. See the point? We know that Real cats can wander at will through time and space, and this cat was probably en route between feeding bowls before it took a wrong turning.

After all, what's the alternative? That Early Man had nothing better to do with his spare time than look at a wild cat and spot that this horizontal-headed, yellow-eyed, spitting menace was just the thing the cave needed? No, our theories demand that it went the other way, that wild cats are domestic cats that went feral thousands of years ago, probably because they were upset about something, possibly the continued non-invention of the fridge.

Cats make ideal time travellers because they can't handle guns. This makes the major drawback of time travel – that you might accidentally shoot your own grandfather – very unlikely. Of course, you might try to *become* your own grandfather, but having watched a family of farm cats, we can tell you that this is perfectly normal behaviour for a cat.

Sex

Well . . .

. . . of course, it all depends how *Real* the cat is,
ifyouseewhatimean . . .

Er . . .

You see, if you have a gentleman cat and a lady cat
who . . .

The point is . . .

In short, pedigree cats breed, Real cats mate.
Breeding is best left to professionals. Mating, on the
other hand, is done by cats.

Breeders seem to be invariably ladies and while
totally mad are nevertheless entirely charming people,
whose houses can be distinguished by the neat sheds
in the garden and the fact that the cat food comes, not
in tins, but in a lorry.

Most Real cat owners seldom if ever encounter
them. It may occasionally happen that they come into
possession of an animal whose looks and history
suggest that she shouldn't be a candidate for the vet's
attentions or those of the huge mad feral tom which
hangs around the garden, and after the expenditure of
a sum of money which makes male members of the

family fantasise about the differences between the cat world and ours, you come back with figures chiming in your head – because you've been told how much the kittens should go for.

Something like: X litters per year × £Y per kitten × save some females × X more litters = ££££!!!!

Real cat owners know that life isn't like that. *Keeping pets for profit is never profitable*, whatever the paperwork says. Life becomes full of rolls of wire netting, feed bills, alfresco carpentry and huge bills from unexpected sources, and your horizons become bounded by, well, the horizon. Who looks after the cattery so that the cattery owner can go on holiday, eh?

In fact, breeding has all been tremendously simplified these days by simply removing the option entirely, to the extent that the 'Free to Good Home' signs seem a lot rarer and a good job too, and the cat population appears to be made up of big fat neutered toms and slim, sleek females whose liberation from the joys of motherhood appears to have come as a bit of a relief. Nevertheless, every neighbourhood still has what is delicately referred to as an Entire Tom.

It is very hard for this animal *not* to be a Real cat. Once upon a time it would have been a tom amongst toms, scrapping and yowling and generally being kept in line by sheer peer pressure. But now all its old mates are fat and lazy and just want to kip all day, whilst the girls don't seem to want to *know*. It stalks

alone through the shrubberies. The ground trembles. Pet rabbits cower in their hutches. Dogs – and, let's be honest, the average dog can be out-thought by even an unReal cat – are so unnerved by its air of make-my-day belligerence that, when they see it coming, they think of dozens of pressing reasons for trotting nonchalantly away. Unpruned and yet unsatisfied, its monstrous Id prowls with it. The milkman complains, the postman starts leaving your letters with the house next door . . .

There was one that took a fiendish delight in fighting all the other local cats. Not over matters of territory, just for the hell of it. It'd creep up while they dozed in the sun, and pitch in.

But we had just got a Real young female at the time. Spayed and scarred, she came from a thriving colony of farm cats so hulking great toms with nothing on their mind except sex and violence, possibly both together, were just part of the scenery as far as she was concerned. The first couple of times the crazed idiot chased her she ran away out of sheer amazement. Then we were privileged to watch the showdown.

It started with the normal attempted mugging and the usual chase and much skidding round corners with *binka-binka-binka* leg pedalling (see 'Cartoon Cats'; every cat has a bit of Cartoon cat in it). Then Real cat scrambled on top of a waterbarrel, waited until the pursuer had his front claws on top and his back legs scrabbling for the purchase necessary to lever his trembling, pear-shaped body the rest of the way, and then with great deliberation hit him across the nose. It was the kind of blow a Cartoon cat would have been proud of; it travelled through 300 degrees, I swear, making a noise like tearing silk.

Then she sat looking at his shocked face with the expression that said he should ask himself whether there was any more where that came from, and was he feeling lucky?

Matters were eventually resolved quite amicably by both animals pretending, as is so often the case when

you meet something you can't do anything about, that the other one didn't exist. This was quite a feat. The tom was a Schrodinger cat who, before being adopted by a neighbour, had come wandering in from whatever hyperspace Schrodinger cats move around in, and for some reason considered that our house was his natural home. Real cat was not going to hiss at him though, because this meant recognising his existence and was therefore against the rules. So the two of them, by some sort of telepathy, made certain that they were never in the same room. It was like those farces when one man is playing twin brothers and is forever running out of the French windows to look for himself just seconds before he walks in via the library door, in a different blazer, cursing at having missed meeting him.

Hygiene

Cats have always had the same well-meaning but shaky grasp of hygiene as humans, viz, if you've covered it over, it isn't there. The important thing is not actually to have achieved Hygiene, but to have been seen to have made the effort – as in, for example, trying to claw the lino into the dirt box.

What's so hygienic about having a wash in your own spit?

However, the Real cat scores over other domestic pets in one unusual respect:

Real cats know what the bathroom is for.

We returned one day to find that the incumbent Real cat, by means of the usual hyperspace travel, had been In when we thought she was Out. Thus no dirt box had been provided.

Real cat, we thought, had a rather shifty expression, although this particular cat has a shifty expression all the time and even breathes as though it is stealing the air. A perfunctory search of the usual resorts of desperation – dark corners, the fireplace –

revealed nothing unpleasant that wasn't normally there.

Until, much later, we went to the bathroom.

More specifically, the bath . . .

You get mixed feelings at a time like this. There is, of course, the feeling of mild admiration that, in a house full of carpets, Real cat has chosen one of the few places that can easily be cleaned by gallons of hot water and an escalation of cleaning fluids (curiously, our book of household hints is definitely reticent about the whole, well, business of cats in the bath). On the other hand, there's the feeling that this is the *bath*, for God's sake, I was really looking forward to a soak and now I will never ever have a bath again as long as I live . . .

What was intriguing was the reaction of other Real cat owners. They said: oh, first time it's happened to you, is it? And went on to tell me about this cat someone heard about who knows how to use the lavatory.

It's bluetits and milk-bottle tops all over again, I tell you. Leave the lid down, that'll fox 'em.

The Real cat on wheels

It's a simple choice. The cat travels either in:

a) a box,

or

b) a stupor.

It's strange that dogs can take a car ride in their stride and still bounce out at the other end, more than ready to widdle, dribble, dig, bite small children and all the other things dogs are good at, while cats find the whole business terribly trying.

Research indicates, however, that a small proportion of Real cats actually like car travel, provided it is on their terms. One of ours was quite at home with the whole thing provided it could sit on the driver's shoulder and watch the road ahead, which is probably against the law.*

*It is: Cats Travelling on Shoulder (Prohibition) Order, 1949.

Animals loose in a car are never a good idea. Goats are generally the worst, but until you realise there's a tortoise stuck under your brake pedal you've never known the meaning of fear, and possibly not the meaning of 'old age' either.

An object lesson in the perils of travelling with a cat was provided by friends who took theirs with them when they moved house.

I know a good game...

It was the last journey – you know, the one where you leave the final key with the neighbours, promise to keep in touch, dig up a few prize plants and set off up the road for the last time with all the things the removal men couldn't or didn't or wouldn't put in the van, like the kids, strange items of kitchen ironmongery, and the cat.

But this was all okay because as far as the cat was concerned a car was just a load of sleeping areas on wheels, and off they went up the motorway, you know the sort of thing, 'Are we nearly there yet?'; 'No you don't feel sick it's just your imagination.'

And then they stopped at a service area.

Really, you don't need to know the rest of the story. You can guess it. But for those who need it spelled out . . .

They forgot about the cat. They got out, they got fed, they got in, they drove another seventy miles, they got out, they started to unpack, there was no cat. Cat must have got out.

Midnight. Car screams into service area car park. Near-hysterical man staggers out with plastic bowl, spoon, lurches around the car park trying to look as nonchalant as is possible concurrent with banging a bowl with a spoon and shouting 'Pusspaws!' in a strained falsetto (he was not, at that time, a paid-up member of the Campaign; if he had been, he'd have been wise to this sort of event and would have changed the cat's name to something like 'Wat!' or 'Zip!')

An hour goes past. Leaves telephone number with least unsympathetic of the waitresses, drives back, visions of family pet laminated to fast lane . . .

Cat leaves it until he's almost home before coming out onto the back seat and yawping for food. With the elderly car so crowded, it'd found a way via the armrest hole into the back of the boot, where it had settled down comfortably behind the spare tyre. But you knew that, anyway.

The Campaign for Real Cats recommends a way to cut through the whole problem of taking cats with you to new homes. It gets rid of all that business of hiding under the bed, peering suspiciously out of the back door, looking betrayed, etc.

The thing is, you see, that your average Real cat becomes attached not to human beings but to routines and territory. It's fashionable to agonise about wives or husbands giving up happy careers to follow the spouse across country, but no one thinks twice about the fact that the family cat may have spent years breaking in dozens of sleeping nests, working out best prowling routes, pouncing places, etc. The human beings around the scene are merely things provided by Nature for, eg, opening fridges and tins. The cat becomes quite *attached* to them, of course. You can become quite attached to a pair of slippers, for that matter. But it is much easier to become attached to new blobs than new sleeping areas.

In short, the Campaign for Real Cats believes that when you move house the kindest thing you can do to the cat is leave it behind, where it will grieve for .003 seconds before sucking up shamefully to the new owners.

As for you, as a catless catlover you will find that a stray turns up outside your new door within days. We think some sort of agency sends them.

The Real cat and other animals

Remember. From the cat's instinctive point of view, the animal world consists of:

1) things that eat it

2) things it can eat

3) things it can eat but will regret immediately; and

4) other cats.

But we then expect it to be perfectly at ease when faced with:

a) Meals On Treadwheels

b) meals in cages (the Flying McNuggets)

c) mad quivering meals in hutches, which in the worst cases may be forced to join our Real cat, plus two dolls and a teddy bear, for a back-lawn tea party consisting of water and crumbled biscuits

d) feathery meals which are actually encouraged to come onto the back lawn for breadcrumbs

e) meals in ponds

f) large grubby barking things

g) miscellaneous.

It's a wonder they stay sane. In fact, as all Real cat owners know, cats get around most problems caused by all of the above by pretending that they don't exist. Just like us, really.

The only household pet I have ever known actually faze a Real cat is a tortoise. This may be because a cat has problems coming to terms with the fact that a tortoise is a fellow fauna. It *appears* to be a small piece of scenery which inexplicably moves about.

These days you don't shove a tortoise in a box to tough it out for the winter, since no one makes tortoises any more and they change hands, people keep telling us, for zillions of pounds. We used to let ours doze the winter away in front of the fire, lurching awake every day or two for a bit of lettuce. A peaceful, untroubled existence, but one which did not appeal to Real cat because a tortoise is impossible to frighten. Tortoises don't know the meaning of the word 'fear' or, indeed, any other word. Oh, they nip into their shell at a passing shadow out of common sense, but as far as they are concerned the presence of a cat in front of the fire just means that here's a pile of fur that is nice

A mobile meat pie??

and warm to burrow under. They sneak up on it, because for tortoises there's no other way, and the first the cat knows is when the edge of a shell is purposefully levering it off the carpet. The cat goes and sits in the corner and looks worried. And then one of them develops an unnatural appetite for cat food. The Real cat sits looking gnomically at a shell seesawing madly on the edge of its dish, and sighs deeply.

The Real cat and
the gardener

Peas, greens, parsnips, rhubarb . . . these are the concerns of your average gardener.

Black thread, twigs, wire netting, incendiary mines . . . these are the concerns of your average gardener who has a Real cat. Or, rather, whose *neighbour* has a Real cat.

It is possible to cultivate your garden when there are Real cats around, but the price of celery is eternal vigilance. As one exasperated Real gardener★ re-

---

★This is not the time and place for extensive definitions. Let's just say that the Real gardener is not the same as the Proper (or Radio) gardener. For example, when the Proper gardener has finished digging, harrowing, sifting, aerating and raking, he has a tilth, possibly even a friable one; when the Real gardener has conscientiously done all these things he has a large heap of stones, roots, twigs and old seed row markers. (Country folk used to believe that certain types of stone were 'mother stones', which gave birth to new stones every year; under *our* garden is a Plastic Seed Row Marker generator.) A Proper gardener has a lawn consisting of Chewings Fescue,

marked, 'It's not just what they Do, it's what they do afterwards', viz, the conscientiously clawed conical heaps, out of which the little yellow shoots of what would have been beans poke pathetically.

The Great Ballistic Clod of Earth has already been touched on. Other possible defences are:

1. The things that rattle, bang, whizz and whirr:

Look, these don't scare *anything*. Well, all right, maybe moles. Come to think of it, we haven't had any

---

Red Bents and Ryegrass; a Real gardener has moss imbedded with dolls' legs, plastic alphabet characters and clothes pegs. And large areas down to Cat.

moles since installing them. We've never had any moles, actually.

2. The Wire Maze:

Real cats step over it.

3. Chemical warfare, including the Mysterious Blobs, the Terrible Dust and the Curious Gungy Stuff:

Since it always rains incessantly immediately this barrage is laid down, we've never found out if any of them work. Anyway, we always feel vaguely uneasy about this sort of thing. Probably there's some international Accord that no one's bothered to tell us about.

The point is that the cat's desire to get onto your pitiful plot is far greater, believe me, than your desire to keep it off. When Nature calls, it shouts. Which leads us on to:

4. The Big Roll of Wire Netting:

The gardener's friend. Watch their Expressions when They Find An Impenetrable Barrier of Steel Laid Above Your Precious Seeds!!!

You can make little wire bootees for the beans, too,

and encase the lower parts of your more valuable apple trees in demure corsets of wire. The snags are 1) a garden that looks like an MoD installation, 2) a tendency to trip up, and 3) the fact that plants grow through the wire. This doesn't matter with things like onions, but we left it too late with the potatoes and they had to be dug up as a unit. But if you can't tolerate this, your only recourse is:

5. The catapult:

But we're not that kind of people.*

*ie, can't aim properly.

The Real cat and children

Ah. They can grow up together.

Well, not really. By the time the average child is no longer doing Winston Churchill impersonations the kitten has grown up and, unless Measures have been Taken, has a family of its own. Kittens and children get on like a house on fire – and just think about what it's actually *like* in a house on fire . . .

A Real kitten in a Real household with a junior member can expect to be:

1) Pulled.

2) Pushed.

3) Imprisoned in Cindy's bedroom with Cindy, Mr T in one of Cindy's dresses*, a one-armed teddy bear, a fearsome Madeofplasticoid with Lazer-zap cannon and a small pink pony.

---

*This sort of thing used to happen all the time in our house. I blame television.

4) Fed unsuitable food. In this category can be included peas, ghastly sweet pink goo, and a fortnight's worth of Kittytreats in three minutes.

5) Inserted into unsuitable clothing (cf. Cindy, Barbie, Action Man, etc.).

6) Carried around by being held in the middle, so that large amounts of cat flop down on either side. (Strangely enough, most cats put up with this, even when they are great fat neutered toms.

It's like all that business with unicorns. Only young maidens can get away with it. The rest of us need stitches.)

It's not that children and young animals get along especially well. It's just that young animals aren't experienced enough to know what's going to happen. Stick to puppies. They're practically child-proof.

The cats we missed

As has been mentioned already, Man has throughout history tried to overcome various deficiencies – his inability to outrun a hare, dig up a badger, bite lumps out of a burglar's behind, carry brandy barrels through deep Alpine snow, etc – by breeding a variety of dog to do it for him. The dog, in fact, has been a kind of handy Plasticine, rolled out thin or squeezed up fat to suit the demands of the time.

Since speculating on what things might be like if history had been different is now thoroughly acceptable in the best scientific circles, the research branch of the Campaign for Real Cats started to wonder what might have happened if dogs hadn't been so handy.

Perhaps there was a great plague, for example, or all dogs were wiped out by a series of devastating but amazingly accurately pinpointed meteor strikes back in the Lower Obscene Age. They also uncovered some early experiments hitherto unheard of.

Winding forward to the new-look Present Day, then, we would have seen:

The Bullmog: Bred originally in the 14th century for the purposes of bull-baiting. However, this was not a very successful experiment and led almost instantly to the virtual extinction of the breed since it could not, when faced with an irate bull, overcome the instinct to jump on it, try to trap it on one paw, throw it in the air, etc.

Smoocher: Something of a mongrel and a favourite with poachers, the Smoocher combines elements of the Eeke, the Bullmog and anything else that happened to be passing and couldn't run away fast enough. It is renowned for its intelligence and cunning. It is so intelligent and cunning, actually, that it is very difficult to get it to do any work at all. Its preferred way of catching rabbits, for example, is to send them a brief note consisting of letters snipped out of newspapers, making them an offer they can't refuse.

King Charles' Lapcat: Familiar to everyone. Note length of ears.

The Eeke: The smallest cat in the world. The Eeke was originally bred as a court pet of the H'sing H'song emperors, and was not introduced to occidental cat fanciers until the 17th century. It was, initially, a toy for high-born ladies but it was soon found to be

The Eeke

extremely useful *since it was the same size as the mice*, and could go down their holes and mug them on the corners.

Mouse-baiting, using trained Eekes, was a popular pastime among the sporting classes for a while. This caused long-term problems, however, since the more intelligent Eekes realised that with the mice wiped out and the walls of an entire manor house at their disposal there was no need to come out.

They are still a nuisance in some parts of the country where, apart from the theft of food, the purring of an entire breeding colony can keep guests awake at night.

The Smog: A cat bred, quite simply, to fight other cats. Owing to an unexplained occurrence of Lamarckian heredity, the Smog lost its ears in the 16th century, its tail – which opponents could hang onto – in the 17th century, and most of its hair in the ring, while its claws and teeth lengthened and toughened. An ordinary cat, going up against a Smog, might as well run into an aeroplane propeller. Good with children.

The Tabby Retriever: Likely to be seen in the back of the kind of cars that are driven by people who wear green wellies and those jerkin things apparently made out of flattened mattresses. Originally a guncat, the

Tabby Retriever was renowned for chasing the quarry, letting it go, chasing it again, pouncing on it, and bringing half of it back to the owner.

THE TABBY RETRIEVER

Dachskatz: An affectionate pet, often referred to as the 'sausage mog'. Popular in the home that can't afford draught excluders. Also, the only cat that can brush up against the front *and* the back of your legs at the same time.

The Pussky: Much used by lazy Eskimos, trappers, Mounties, etc. Refuses to go out in cold weather.

The Snufflecat: This breed came into its own in the American South, when it was used to track escaped slaves and convicts, who were very lucky escaped convicts and slaves indeed because, although the Snufflecat has a superb sense of smell, it doesn't know what to do with it.

The St Eric: Many a weary traveller, half-buried in the snow, has hauled himself out and kept himself warm at the sheer rage of seeing a St Eric curl up and go to sleep twenty yards away. They were never a great success, since they depended on a cat's natural sense of charity and benevolence . . .

The German Sheepcat: Never very good with sheep, actually, but a great favourite with police departments across the world. The cat's natural tendency to rub up against people has, in these 150lb specimens, become a desire to smash open doors and knock people to the floor, where they are drooled on.

(The most famous German Sheepcat was the film star *RanCanCan*, who had a spectacular if somewhat brief career in the 1940s. Faced with bridges being washed away ahead of speeding express trains, or fire breaking out in tall orphanages, or people being lost in ancient mine workings, RanCanCan could be relied upon to wander off and look for something to eat. But very, very photogenically.)

The future of the Real cat

If you're prepared to accept the Schrodinger theory, then it is rosy – in fact, the last man on Earth will probably look out of his bunker and find a cat sitting there patiently waiting for the fridge to be opened.

Actually, theories don't come into it. Real cats are survivalists. They've got it down to a fine art. What other animal gets fed, not because it's useful, or guards the house, or sings, but because when it *does* get fed it looks pleased? And purrs. The purr is very important. It's the purr that does it every time. It's the purr that makes up for the Things Under the Bed, the occasional pungency, the 4 a.m. yowl. Other creatures went in for big teeth, long legs or over-active brains, while cats just settled for a noise that tells the world they're feeling happy. The purr ought to have been a pair of concrete running shoes in the great race of evolution; instead, it gave cats a rather better deal than most animals can expect, given Mankind's fairly unhappy record in his dealings with his fellow creatures. Cats learned to evolve in a world designed initially by nature but in practice by humans, and have got damn good at it. The purr means 'make me happy and I'll make *you* happy'. The advertising industry took centuries to cotton on to that beguiling truth, but when it did, it sold an awful lot of Cabbage Patch dolls.

You've got to hand it to Real cats.

If you don't, they wait until your back is turned and take it anyway.

It's nice to think, though, that if the future turns out to be not as bad as people forecast, ie, if it actually even *exists*, then among the domes and tubes of some orbiting colony, hundreds of years from now, dynamic people with sturdy chins, people who know all about mining asteroids and stuff like that, will still be standing outside their biomodule banging a plastic plate with a spoon.

And yelling 'Zut!' or 'Wip!', if they've got any sense.